Land of the Dragons

Rod Morris

Learning Media

Contents

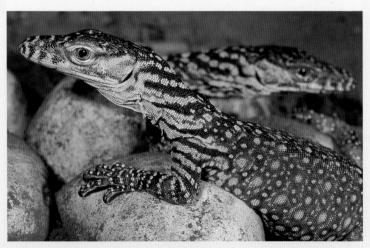

Chapter 1

"What's this?" my daughter Rachel asked one day. She had carried a large brown carving into the room. It looked a bit like a crocodile with its mouth slightly open. "Is it a crocodile?" she asked.

I told her it was a dragon from Indonesia. It was carved for me by my friend Nuhung. It looks very old and has amazing red and black eyes made from raintree seeds.

"I used to collect the seeds for Nuhung so that the dragons he made could see."

"This dragon must be very old," Rachel said.

"Oh, it's not really old," I replied, "but the story that goes with this dragon goes back a very long time."

A long time ago, before Nuhung was born, before his village was even there, men wandered round the island hunting and fishing. In those days, there were no women on the island. The men had all been sent there as a punishment by the Sultan of Bima, a powerful ruler who lived on another island nearby.

Years passed, and the sultan heard that the men had banded together and learned to live by helping each other. The sultan was so impressed that he sent the men wives. In time, one of the women gave birth to twins, a little boy and a little girl – but the little boy was born a cripple. Life for the parents became difficult. They had to travel about to find food, and this was difficult to do with their son the way he was. The next time they moved on, they decided to leave him in a clearing in the forest.

7

After many years, more children were born, and the people settled down and built a little village, or kampung, near the coast. They called it Kampung Komodo. The little girl was now a young woman, but she had never forgotten that she had a little brother. One day, in a clearing near the village, she met a crippled dragon. "This is my long-lost brother," she thought, and she ran back to the village to get some food for him. Others heard the news of the dragon and brought food to the clearing for him too. It wasn't long before the dragon came right into the village to be fed.

"What a lovely story," said Rachel, "but what a pity that dragons aren't real."

"Oh, but they are," I said. "In Nuhung's village, there are real live dragons. They walk about as if they own the place. I know, because I've seen them."

Chapter 2

***N**uhung still lives on the island of Komodo. When I first met him, he had nine children and nine grandchildren. As they grew up, he told each of them the story of the dragon.

Sometimes, when the fishermen put out their fish to dry in the sun, the smell will bring a dragon out of the forest. So the fishermen have to watch their catch very carefully.

There are special tricks to learn when you are living with dragons. You can't tie up your dogs or keep your pigs or chickens in a pen. A dragon might catch them and eat them! You have to be careful in the sea too. Komodo dragons are good swimmers.

Komodo dragons are just as fierce as the dragons you read about in storybooks. They are the world's biggest lizard. A big male Komodo dragon can be over ten feet long. There are over three thousand of these giant lizards living on Komodo – they are really the rulers of the island. They can hunt and kill anything – deer, pigs, goats. On another island nearby called Rincha, they hunt monkeys. But the real test of a Komodo dragon's strength is when it hunts down an enormous water buffalo.

When this happens, there is too much food for one dragon, so you get a dragon feast. Komodos have a very good sense of smell. They use their yellow forked tongues to taste the air. If they smell something that's been killed, they will come from miles around to check it out.

Komodo dragons have very sharp teeth. They are very good at cutting up and eating animals they have killed. Some people believe that Komodo dragons eat the same way that the meat-eating dinosaurs did, so they are very special lizards.

Chapter 3

*T*he most exciting time to be on Komodo is at courtship time, when the big male dragons are fighting for a mate. That's when I saw my first crippled dragon.

The males chase each other around. When two of the males meet, they stand face to face and try to make each other turn away. Then they hiss loudly and puff themselves up to look bigger. They stand up on their back legs and fight like wrestlers, trying to push each other over.

The winner pushes the other dragon over and holds him down. He scratches him again and again with his strong sharp claws. That shows that he's the winner.

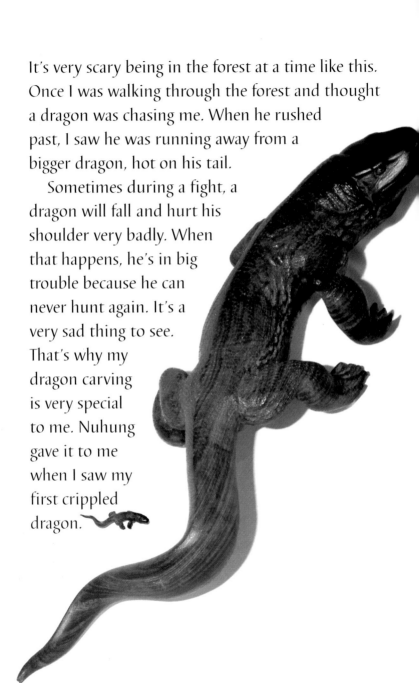

It's very scary being in the forest at a time like this. Once I was walking through the forest and thought a dragon was chasing me. When he rushed past, I saw he was running away from a bigger dragon, hot on his tail.

Sometimes during a fight, a dragon will fall and hurt his shoulder very badly. When that happens, he's in big trouble because he can never hunt again. It's a very sad thing to see. That's why my dragon carving is very special to me. Nuhung gave it to me when I saw my first crippled dragon.

Chapter 4

In some ways, Komodo dragons are like the dragons you find in fairytales. Their "flickering" yellow tongue does look a little bit like fire. They like living in holes, just like the fire-breathing dragons in storybooks. They also look after a special kind of "buried treasure."

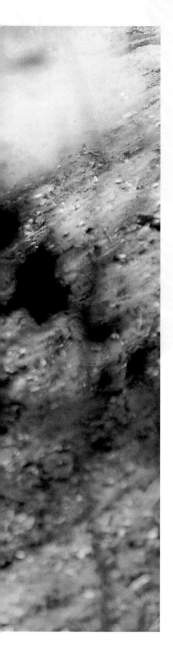

Before I went to the island of Komodo, nobody had ever found a Komodo dragon's nest with eggs in it. I wanted to look for one, and Nuhung's brother gave me a good clue. He said that a female dragon had chased him away from a place she was watching very carefully.

He also saw her chase away a pig, a deer, and a male dragon from the same place. So one day I followed a female dragon. She kept going back to a big pile of earth in a quiet part of the forest. The pile of earth had been made by a pair of birds called mound builders, to lay their eggs in. But at that time of the year, the birds were not using it. Maybe the dragon was going to lay her eggs there too.

Each day the dragon went to the mound and lay down in the sun. Sometimes she dug small holes in it. Then one day she dug a huge hole and crawled inside. After half a day, she came back out and filled the hole in. Had she laid her eggs? She did look a lot thinner.

She stayed in the bushes by the mound. She even slept there at night. Whenever other females came near, she gave a loud hiss and chased them away. She was a dragon watching over buried treasure. The treasure was twenty-two dragon eggs. How do I know? Because when I went back nine months later, I counted the empty shells!

Chapter 5

1 watched the female dragon guarding her nest for three more weeks. Then I had to leave the island. A ranger called Matius watched the nest for me while I was gone.

He told me later that the dragon had guarded her nest for two more months. Then she had gone off into the forest.

When I came back to the island in the warmer weather, I went quickly to find the dragon's nest again. The female was nowhere to be seen. Matius and I started to dig to find the buried treasure – dragons' eggs! We dug out the soft earth from the tunnel that the dragon had made nine months before.

At first, we couldn't find anything. Maybe she hadn't laid any eggs after all. Then some soil fell away, and I saw some empty eggs ... and twenty-two baby dragons! They already had tiny teeth as sharp as knives. Matius and I were so excited. This was the first time anyone had seen this happen.

We carefully covered in the nest again so that the babies would be safe. By the next day, some of them had already dug their way back out of the nest. They must have been very strong diggers. They stopped to have a quick look around, and then they scampered away and climbed into the trees.

Baby Komodo dragons stay up in the trees until they are eighteen months old. It's safer for them up there, with so many hungry adult dragons on the ground.

Adult dragons are too heavy to climb trees, but the young ones are very good climbers. They have long toes and sharp claws for holding on to branches.

"If the Komodo dragon is the biggest lizard in the world," said Rachel, "I wonder what the smallest one is?"

"Well," I said, "the smallest lizard in the world lives on another island called Madagascar. That dragon is smaller than the end of your little finger."

"Have you seen it?" she asked.

"Yes, I've seen it," I said, "but that's another story!"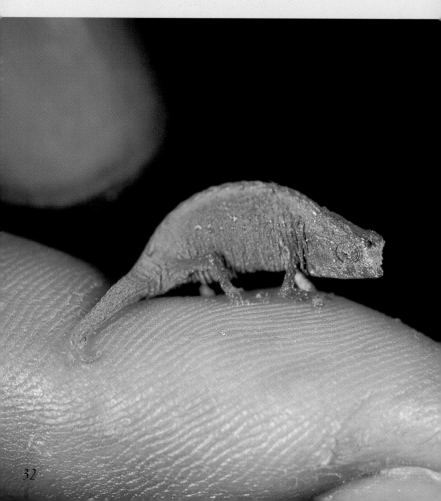